SEARS TOWER

A BUILDING BOOK FROM
THE CHICAGO
ARCHITECTURE FOUNDATION

JAY PRIDMORE

PHOTOGRAPHS BY
HEDRICH BLESSING

Pomegranate

SAN FRANCISCO

Published by Pomegranate Communications, Inc.
Box 6099, Rohnert Park, California 94927
800 277 1428; www.pomegranate.com

Pomegranate Europe Ltd.
Fullbridge House, Fullbridge
Maldon, Essex CM9 4LE, England

Library of Congress Cataloging-in-Publication Data

Pridmore, Jay,

    Sears Tower : a building book from the Chicago Architecture Foundation/Jay Pridmore.

        p. cm.

    ISBN 0-7649-2021-9

      1. Sears Tower (Chicago, Ill.) 2. Architecture—Illinois—Chicago—20th century. 3.
Skyscrapers—Illinois—Chicago. 4. Office buildings—Illinois—Chicago. 5. Skidmore,
Owings & Merrill. 6. Chicago (Ill.)—Buildings, structures, etc. I. Chicago Architecture
Foundation. II. Title.

NA6233.C4 S436 2002
720'.483'097311—dc21

                                     2001054881

Pomegranate Catalog No. A625

Cover and book design by Lynn Bell, Monroe Street Studios, Santa Rosa, CA

Printed in Korea

10 09 08 07 06 05 04 03 02   10 9 8 7 6 5 4 3 2 1

Mission

The Chicago Architecture Foundation (CAF) is dedicated to advancing public interest and education in architecture and related design. CAF pursues this mission through a comprehensive program of tours, lectures, exhibitions, special programs, and youth programs, all designed to enhance the public's awareness and appreciation of Chicago's important architectural legacy.

Founded in 1966, the Chicago Architecture Foundation has evolved to become a nationally recognized resource advancing public interest and education in Chicago's outstanding architecture. Its programs serve more than 250,000 people each year. For more information contact us at the address below, or visit us on our website:

Chicago Architecture Foundation
224 South Michigan Avenue
Chicago IL 60604
319-922-TOUR (8687)
www.architecture.org

SEARS TOWER

Sears Tower was named for Sears, Roebuck & Company, and was topped out May 3, 1973. The Tower then became the world's tallest building at 1,454 feet, surpassing the previous record holder, the World Trade Center in Manhattan, which was completed in 1972 and reached 1,368 feet in height. Before that, the Empire State Building, built in 1931 and topping out at 1,250 feet, held the record. Today, the Petronas Towers in Kuala Lampur, Malaysia, are taller than Sears Tower, but only because of their decorative spires, which rise 1,483 feet from the ground. Sears Tower remains the tallest building in the world by at least two measures: (1) the highest occupied floor level (110th floor) and (2) the highest skyscraper roof.

SEARS TOWER STATISTICS

Architect/Engineer:	Skidmore, Owings & Merrill
Cost:	$175 million
Size of site:	3 acres, bounded by Adams and Franklin Streets, Jackson Boulevard, and Wacker Drive.
Total area:	440 million square feet, surpassed only by the Pentagon
Number of stories:	110
Largest floors:	1 through 49, each approximately 50,000 square feet
Foundation:	114 concrete piles sunk an average of 100 feet and into limestone bedrock
Structure and materials:	bundled-tube construction with steel, concrete, anodized aluminum, and bronze-tinted glass
Number of elevators:	104, including 14 double-deckers that carry passengers to the sky lobbies on the 33rd and 34th and the 66th and 67th floors, where people can then transfer to local elevators
Weekday population:	approximately 16,500 people work in Sears Tower daily
Skydeck:	located on 103rd floor with a total area of 11,000 square feet and views of four states: Illinois, Indiana, Wisconsin, Michigan
Window cleaning:	6 roof-mounted robotic window washing machines clean the Tower's 16,100 windows

Great buildings, like all great landmarks, define themselves. The Grand Canyon and Niagara Falls are both breathtaking for reasons of their own. So it is with Sears Tower—still the tallest building in the world by several measures—whose engineers and architects built a functional office building and at the same time climbed to the top of the world.

Sears Tower remains the world's most famous skyscraper from an era when soaring skyscrapers were the great hope of American cities. It was the world's tallest building at 1,454 feet, and also the world's largest private building, with 4.5 million square feet. Today, those records may (or may not) have been surpassed. What has not changed is the lasting impression Sears Tower continues to make. From the time it was designed, it was a case study for engineers. As a tourist attraction, it grows with each succeeding year. And as a proud icon on the Chicago skyline, it stands as a stunning human achievement.

The building has had its critics. "Mega-skyscrapers will only aggravate urban congestion," cried some when Sears Tower went up. Others complained that its gargantuan interiors were too large, too cavernous for proper offices. And while a journalist of the *Chicago Tribune* applauded the sheer bravado of Sears Tower, he could not keep from adding that "the uppermost section seems out of scale with the lower stories."

But history has survived the doubters. For one, Sears Tower has only enhanced its corner of the West Loop, where it transformed a neighborhood of

Photograph © Hedrich Blessing

Sears Tower varies in profile and character from almost every direction and every time of day. Seen here from the southwest, its setbacks display big shoulders that sometimes dwarf its neighbors.

From the east (past Phillip Johnson's postmodern 190 South LaSalle Street), Sears Tower's profile (above) resembles a campanile. After dark, it serves the city as a beacon of light.

Photograph © Hedrich Blessing

warehouses and tailor shops into a commercial epicenter. And its 50,000-square foot floors, while grudging of natural light, are rich in the clear-span space that contemporary designers and efficient managers prefer. As for the aesthetic question, Sears Tower quite simply established a standard all its own. Saying its proportions are wrong is like claiming that George Washington's nose on Mount Rushmore is too big.

The Genesis

The city's skyscrapers are "Chicago's mountains," some say, but Sears Tower was not an act of nature. It is a building that represents—as major buildings do—the culmination of urban trends and social forces. Some factors tap deep into Chicago's past, such as the story of the world's first skyscraper, William Le Baron Jenney's Home Insurance Building, that went up in 1886 only two blocks from Sears. Other factors are practical, such as the straightening of the Chicago River in 1929, an engineering feat that corrected an inconvenient bend in the river along with a tangle of short streets and rail yards. The construction of South Wacker Drive, Union Station, and the post office were among the immediate results, although many tracts remained undeveloped 40 years later, awaiting a major project to transform them.

That major project appeared when Sears Roebuck & Co., the largest retailer in the nation, resolved to move its headquarters downtown. Since 1904, the company had occupied an enormous complex on Chicago's West Side, created

The view from the Skydeck illustrates how architects have transformed Chicago's native topography into a place of towering promontories and outlooks.

Photograph © Hedrich Blessing

For boaters as well as motorists, Sears Tower is a primary point of reference.

Photograph © Hedrich Blessing

Just as the Tower changes its appearance from different vantage points below, its view from the top provides a rich panorama in every direction. Four states—Illinois, Indiana, Wisconsin, and Michigan—are visible from the Skydeck on a clear day.

as a state-of-the art mail order house, with warehouses, conveyors, loading docks, and a fourteen-story office tower. Like so many things about Sears, this was considered "the biggest" commercial facility in the world. But things had changed since the end of World War II. The buildings had become outdated, and the company was converting obsolete warehouses into sorely needed office space. The neighborhood, moreover, was in the middle of one of America's most battle-scarred urban ghettos. So by the late 1960s, when Sears Chairman Gordon Metcalf resolved to leave the West Side for more modern climes, the only questions were how far away and how fast.

Answering those questions occupied the remainder of Metcalf's chairman-ship and involved the calculations of architects, engineers, real estate brokers, and many others engaged in a project that quickly, but not immediately, grew to its unprecedented scale. In 1970, Metcalf announced the creation of Sears Tower: "Being the largest retailer in the world," he said, "we thought we should have the largest headquarters in the world." Metcalf's declaration was only half true; the plans for Sears's new headquarters were not originally the tallest any-thing because they were conceived not by master builders but by storekeepers, who planned this building like they planned their stores: from the inside out.

In fact, Sears Roebuck had no idea what their building would look like until well after an interior design firm called Environetics, self-described (appropri-ately, under the circumstances) as "the largest in the world," devised a detailed plan for the store. To begin, Environetics interviewed ninety-five

From Grant Park, a tableaux of Chicago architecture includes
Sears Tower flanked by Willoughby Tower (left, 1929) and
the First National Bank (now Bank One) Building (1969).

Photograph © Hedrich Blessing

Sears department heads, assessed their needs, projected their growth, and presented conclusions that were surprisingly explicit. Their dominant conclusion was that Sears needed approximately 2 million square feet immediately; more speculative was the projection that thirty years down the road they would need twice that space. Within those parameters, the design firm divined that optimal floor size was 50,000 square feet. All these factors led to the conclusion that Sears would build a very big glass box, and maybe two.

To the West Loop

What the interior designers could not say was where the building ought to go. That decision fell to Sear's senior management, which diligently shopped for more than a year for the right real estate. To be safe, they considered other sites—but the front-runner was always downtown Chicago. This area represented, partially, Sears's loyalty to the city where it had become America's "Big Store," as it was called affectionately and otherwise. Mostly the Loop and its immediate environs were targeted by the real estate market. For a generation, Chicago had been changing from factory center to financial crossroads. In response, Mayor Richard J. Daley had lifted many zoning restrictions in the city's Loop, including previously strict constraints on height. By the 1960s the market for downtown office space was escalating rapidly along with major skyscraper projects, and among changes to the skyline were the John Hancock Center and the Standard Oil Building, that were to be completed in 1970 and 1973, respectively.

Sears was eager to be a part of the modern city—but not before it engaged in some old fashioned horse trading to settle there. In Chicago, buying land has never been simple, and in charge of negotiations was Sears's vice president for real estate, Warren Skoning, a plain-spoken and well-liked executive. Skoning's first serious flirtation reportedly was for a site with air rights over the Illinois Central tracks near Michigan Avenue and Roosevelt Road. There were nearly a dozen other possibilities as well, all marked on a large map of Chicago in Skoning's office. But Metcalf was unsold until Skoning agreed to one more offer in mid-1968. This offer came from James Peters, a brash New Yorker with Cushman & Wakefield, the largest (naturally) real estate broker in the country. Peters had recently discussed Sears with his friend Al Taubman, a major shopping center developer who had worked with Skoning for years. Taubman told Peters that Sears was looking, and Peters had sellers with something that just might appeal: a substantial lot on the east side of South Wacker Drive.

Peters quickly flew to Chicago, and Skoning was interested, but he noted that Sears's space needs were greater than the property in question. The store needed a full city block at least, he said, whereupon Peters went back to the

Sears Tower was sited with a view for accessibility by more than 7,000 Sears employees. In what had been less-than-central downtown real estate, the Tower created new energy in the West Loop near the expressway's "spaghetti bowl" interchange, the commuter rail lines, and the old residential areas (facing page) that make Chicago the "city of neighborhoods."

sellers and told them that if they bought what remained on the block between Adams Street and Jackson Boulevard, their investment might quickly pay off. They agreed and succeeded, and a few months later, despite a potentially troublesome small street through the middle of the property, and despite a hard final night of negotiations, the 3-acre site went for a reported $11 million.

A Design of Poetry and Economy

Sears next brought on James Peters's brother, Anthony Peters, a Cushman & Wakefield consultant, who quickly involved himself with planning, pricing, and finding the right architects for the building, which no one yet Imagined would be a "tower." Peters sought serious proposals from five firms, four of them from Chicago, and before the end of 1969 recommended Skidmore, Owings & Merrill. SOM, as it was called, was considered the leading specialist in cost-efficient and often striking corporate buildings, and the emphasis was on cost efficiency. "Sears wasn't interested in building a monument," Peters said. "They wanted to build something that was economical."

Indeed, SOM was driven by the principle made famous by Mies van der Rohe, the father of postwar modernism. Mies's theory of modern skyscraper design, practiced most faithfully in Chicago, where the German architect had settled before World War II, had been reduced to the slogan "less is more." To admirers and followers at SOM this meant less structural steel and less materials of all kinds, an aesthetic, to be sure, but also a means of keeping

Once a city of smoke and stockyards, Chicago was transformed after World War II into a great commercial center with an escalating need for massive office buildings and great skyscrapers.

Photograph © Hedrich Blessing

construction costs as low as possible. "Less is more" also meant more space with minimal structural impediments inside—"clear-span" space, as it was called, regarded as a great advantage for interior planning. For most of the postwar period, SOM had also succeeded in creating some of the most open and flexible interiors, in addition to some of the most stately buildings, in the great economic boom of postwar America. In Chicago these structures included the Inland Steel Building (1958) and later the John Hancock Center on Michigan Avenue.

The earliest schemes for Sears were not stately, however. Rather, they consisted of a large glass box, or two of them, connected by a bridge. These seemed like functional solutions, yet SOM architects, including design partner Bruce Graham, still had visions of a tall building, and it was not long before the client was aspiring in that direction as well. One obstacle to this frankly more spectacular approach was the small public thoroughfare on the property, Quincy Street, which would have to be eliminated to make room for a major skyscraper. So Sears moved to buy it, and although such a proposition is normally easier said than done in any city, Chicago's Mayor Richard J. Daley demonstrated his own love of skyscrapers by sidestepping political discussion with the City Council and selling Quincy Street to Sears for a price that made the store's counting room smile.

Fazlur Khan's Framed-Tube Construction

While most clients chose SOM for economy engineering, some chose them for the poetry of their architecture. By now Sears was interested in both, and the firm was just then in the forefront of putting together the prosaic and the poetic through a technique called framed-tube construction. This building type was based on the principle that a structural frame, with additional support around the perimeter, constituted a "tube" of adequate strength to support the building without the maze of interior columns necessary in conventional skyscrapers (such as the Empire State Building). These loads were known to be particularly formidable because the pressures of gravity are accompanied by the pressure of wind, increasingly severe on buildings above seventy stories. At SOM and other major firms, these insights, along with early computer programs, were showing engineers that framed tube construction used less steel, produced larger interior spans, and made skyscrapers more economical than ever.

SOM's leading proponent of the tube construction was its chief engineer, Fazlur Khan, a former Fulbright scholar from Bangladesh. Khan and designer Bruce Graham embarked on the Sears project just as another framed-tube skyscraper was going up, the John Hancock Center, with its system of diagonal

Chicago's ceiling is held up by its three greatest skyscrapers (left to right):
John Hancock, Sears Tower, and the Standard Oil (now Aon) Building.

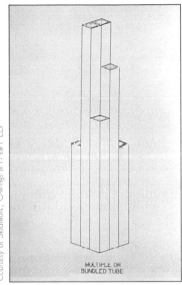

Courtesy of Skidmore, Owings & Merrill LLP

MULTIPLE OR
BUNDLED TUBE

Skidmore, Owings & Merrill pio
neered the use of computers in com-
puter-assisted design (CAD).
While engineers mostly studied
reams of numerical printouts to cal-
culate loads, they also provided
clear visualizations of the Tower's
bundled-tube construction.

Courtesy of Skidmore, Owings & Merrill LLP

braces to reinforce and lighten the weight of the structure. Hancock was nearly complete and already an economical and aesthetic success when Sears hired SOM. The client did not want a copy of the tapered John Hancock, but it did want an expression just as modern and just as distinctive. Both Graham and Khan were eager to oblige.

Their answer for Sears Tower came one afternoon at the Chicago Club, where the two SOM partners were having lunch. Discussing the Sears project, Khan observed that a cluster of tubes, with each tube sharing walls and helping to support those adjacent to it, appeared to be a most efficient solution for such a large building, although he admitted it might be less than sleek. Graham frowned and looked down at his pack of cigarettes and was about to reach for one when a thought struck him. The architect took out a handful of Camels, held them in his fist, and showed them to Khan. Each cigarette rose to a different height, and Khan understood immediately.

The scheme was essentially worked out that afternoon. The lower section of the tower, with all nine tubes (75 feet square) rising forty-nine stories in height, would accommodate Sears's current needs. Here, Sears got its 50,000-square foot floors; above were smaller floors where Sears could expand in the future but rent for the time being. Khan and Graham's bundled tubes, therefore, met several overriding requirements: it gave Sears 1½-acre floors; it rendered the

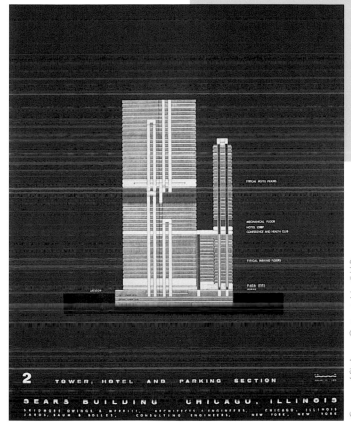

SOM created a number of schemes before the 110-story tower was agreed upon.
One possibility included an attached hotel since enough Sears employees from
other locations were often visiting to keep a good-sized hotel fully occupied.

building's handsome set-back profile; and it enhanced the rentability of smaller upper floors with more windows and more corner offices per square foot.

As the solution developed, SOM calculated that Sears's current and future needs would bring the height of the tower to ninety-five stories, perhaps a few more. The architects quickly realized that this measurement was not many stories short of the World Trade Center (designed by Minoru Yamasaki and Emery Roth & Sons), then under construction, which was to break the world height record at 1,368 feet. The possibility of making Sears Tower the world's tallest building excited the architects and interested Sears Chairman Metcalf nearly as much, whereupon SOM presented a new scheme, something close to the final one, that reached 1,454 feet, which was the absolute limit because of FAA regulations. A few weeks later, Metcalf unveiled a model for the new Sears Tower and told the press that the biggest store in the world could have nothing less than the tallest building.

Construction

Ground was broken in June 1971, beginning one of the most extraordinary projects that anyone involved had ever experienced. It was a fast-track project because Sears was anxious to move, and interest rates on the $175 million needed for the construction were high and getting higher. Fast track meant that many design decisions were made while work was in progress. Some of these were minor details, other less minor, and at least one was fundamental to the way the building would look: the material on the outside walls.

Courtesy of American Bridge Company.

Iron workers assembled the Tower's frame in prefabricated sections that the crew called Christmas trees, named because they were 25-foot columns with spandrels branching off.

Architect Graham had always envisioned Sears Tower as black. "A steel building should be black," he said. But the preferred material to achieve the effect, anodized aluminum, was manufactured at that time by only one vendor, whose price was far higher than expected and threatened to break Sears's budget. This problem was unresolved when Graham and Richard Halpern, director of Diesel Construction, the general contractor, were touring a granite facility in Italy. While they were outside Rome shopping for paving stone for the exterior plaza, they quickly learned that the Italians were eager to sell granite for the Tower's outside walls as well, and would do so economically. In fact, the idea of granite shook Graham's modernist sensibility—stone covering steel seemed like oil and water to an architect who believed that honest form resided only in the pure representation of building materials. Fortunately, the aluminum manufacturer was unfamiliar with Graham's ideology, and when salesmen heard rumors of Graham and Halpern's Roman visit, they swiftly brought the aluminum price to within Sears's budget.

Downbidding the aluminum was just one improvisation that Richard Halpern and his staff, including superintendent Ray Worley, engineered in the 3½ years it took to build Sears Tower. Many construction techniques were new, and none had been used on such a scale. Structural units called "Christmas trees" were 25-foot-high columns with 15-foot sections of spandrel prefabricated and hoisted in place. Assembly was achieved with four "creeper derricks" lifted by winches and remounted four stories at a time. These and other

Courtesy of American Bridge Company

The Tower's steel structure rose at a rate of eight stories a month—
an intensive process that employed a system of "creeper derricks."

Building the world's largest commercial building required constant communications for contractors and crews using a hotel-style Centrex telephone system.

One of the logistical requirements of constuction was getting "Christmas trees" to the work site in such a manner that deliveries did not contribute to a downtown traffic nightmare.

Chicago architecture was known for its truthful expression of a building's structure. To local architects especially there was something beautiful about a steel frame that was as simple as it was massive.

Courtesy of Skidmore,
Owings & Merrill LLP

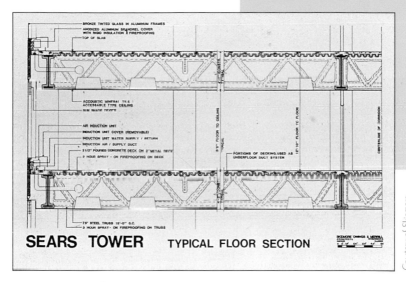

Opposite: As Chicago watched the structural steel go up, the fireproofing get applied,
and exterior walls go in, it was an object lesson in modern construction.

Above: Joists were prepared to support floors of poured concrete. Three ducts were built
into each floor, one for electricity, one for telephones, and a third for other technology at a
time when Sears was making itself ready for the cybernetic future, whatever it might be.

From the beginning of the project in 1971, the construction of Sears Tower represented a logistical feat as well as a technological one. The people involved compared its size, scope, and intensity to the pyramids of Egypt.

Courtesy of Skidmore, Owings & Merrill LLP

Even in an incomplete stage of construction, the proportions
of Sears Tower suggested the soaring skyscraper still to come.

Photograph © Hedrich Blessing

When completed in 1974, the base of Sears Tower was stark and uncompromising, expressive of its utter regularity and the purity of its steel structure and granite plaza. Planters provided some human-scale comforts to the base, which were otherwise lacking when the modernist masterwork was completed. Changes were to come, however.

contrivances were designed in a project that, some said, required the same ingenuity and patience to build as the pyramids.

Structural technologies, too, were refined by suppliers and then mastered by tradespeople. A special drywall system, for example, employed slip joints to compensate for the inevitable sway of the building (reduced but not eliminated by the bundled-tube design); without this system, interior walls might rip apart in a storm. Mechanical systems were created on world-record scale, including an elevator system with 104 cars (some double-deckers), with expresses to transfer points called sky lobbies at the 33rd and 34th floors via double-decked cars, then at the 66th and 67th floors.

The World's Tallest Building was topped off in ceremonies on a frigid spring day, May 3, 1973. Mayor Daley and Cardinal Cody joined thousands of Sears employees in autographing the final beam before it was bolted in place. The building opened the following fall when Sears undertook another corporate superlative: the biggest move in American business history.

Adapting to Times

In the decades since it opened, Sears Tower has become a lightning rod for change and sometimes subject to controversy. In the 1970s and 1980s, climbers tried to scale it, each time getting into a bitter altercation with police. In early 1984, the Tower was refitted with a new entrance, a design that generated more architectural debate than any new doorway in recent memory. Then

Courtesy of Skidmore, Owings & Merrill LLP

By 1984, when the new Wacker Drive entry was planned, SOM's strict modernism had softened to permit a dramatically curved glass ceiling. The renovation provided some of the theatricality that many felt was appropriate for an entrance to the World's Tallest Building.

Sculptor Alexander Calder created *Universe* for Sears Tower, a mobile of varied shapes, colors, and movements suggesting the infinite potential of human creativity.

Designed by SOM, the new entryway was nicknamed "the lunch box" by some other architects. The sweeping stairs are now gone, but then as now the addition rendered a more dramatic sense of arrival to a building that merited more street level prominence than the architects originally designed.

Photograph © Hedrich Blessing

The basic character of Sears Tower as a practical and economical building was established in the beginning. While many of its tenants have fashioned a measure of luxury in their rented quarters, the standard architecture of the Tower has not been transformed and calls for a simplicity that reflected the character of Sears Roebuck and the essence of the building.

Photograph © Hedrich Blessing

Never had such a large interior been so scientifically laid out. Designers spent months studying the work and customary flow of Sears employees before creating highly functional work spaces in the first forty-nine stories of the Tower.

Time and motion studies were made of Sears before the 1974 move to determine the ideal location for various departments and how they should be laid out. From bottom to top—with the exception of the most senior executives—offices were built for efficiency, not luxury, and standard issue furnishings were de rigueur.

In the open spaces of Sear's 50,000-square foot floors, robotic mail carriers were not only desirable, they were also possible. Roof-mounted, robotically controlled, window washers (facing page) were also installed to keep black aluminum walls and more than 16,000 windows clean.

Photograph © Hedrich Blessing

Lobbies at Sears Tower are exquisitely modernist, with transparent walls and escalators piercing vertical space. Early 1990s renovation by De Stefano & Partners offended some purists with elaborate finishes, but these changes, which kept pace with the times, more importantly emphasized the sheer size of the modern skyscraper and its interior space.

Photograph © Hedrich Blessing

When SOM planned Sears Tower's new entrance in the early 1980s, the objective was to provide a more dramatic presence on a street that the building itself had transformed. South Wacker Drive, once a mere appendage to the Loop, became an up-to-date financial and commercial center.

Sears Tower Skydeck has been one of Chicago's most popular tourist attractions at least since the 1985 renovation of the street-level entrances and the 103rd floor. On a clear day, the view is of four states and the architectural center of America.

Photograph © Hedrich Blessing

in the late 1980s, Sears Roebuck decided to relocate its entire headquarters operation to a new campus in Chicago's suburb of Hoffman Estates. It was a move that made some wonder if the World's Tallest was not a white elephant.

Clearly, Sears Tower has adapted to the times, largely because of elements of SOM's original architecture as well as to more renovations. Certainly, many modern features of the 1970s are paying handsome dividends today, most emphatically the wide spans of unencumbered interior space, enabling new tenants to design rental offices to exact needs. In an era focused on productivity, moreover, 50,000-square foot floors now suit many financial operations, some with large trading floors, others that require maximum flexibility in office space. Particularly farsighted was Sears's original decision to overdesign sub-floor ductwork. In 1974, they could not predict the technologies of the future, but they left more than ample space for the wiring. Now Sears Tower accommodates modern infrastructure and networks as capable as many "smart" buildings of the 1990s.

Ironically, Sears Tower's success was partially responsible for Sears Roebuck's decision to leave it. Indeed, Sears had changed its West Loop neighborhood permanently for the better. The Big Store, which was suffering new competition and downturns in the 1980s, resolved to concentrate on retailing, not real estate. In 1989 they mortgaged and then sold the Tower, built at a cost of $175 million in 1974, for at least five times that figure in a series of transactions that were complete in 1994.

One of the earliest tenants of Sears Tower, the law offices of Sonnenschein, Rosenthal & Nath has maintained the modernist approach to interior design that Sears Tower suggested from the beginning. A 1995 renovation of the offices displayed touches of elegance but retained the utilitarian function of Sears Tower and the democratic spirit of the Sonnenschein firm.

An American Icon

Under the ownership of TrizecHahn Office Properties, Sears Tower's reputation as an American icon has only increased—even after the potentially demoralizing effect of the Petronas Towers in Malaysia rising a few feet higher, and even after the collapse of the towers of the World Trade Center. Sears Tower has endured not just as a symbol of a corporation or of an architectural firm or even of a single city. Now more than ever, it is a timeless monument to American courage and ingenuity.

In the twenty-first century, the Tower represents some of Chicago's most desirable commercial real estate, with law firms, investment houses, and other companies of a stature that makes 233 South Wacker Drive an address of worldwide prestige. Sears Tower also has assumed a position as one of Chicago's most popular tourist attractions. Architects and structural engineers never tire of describing it, and longtime Chicagoans frequently recall what they were doing when it was built. Sears Tower is both an urban landmark and a cultural milestone.

Some qualities are as ineffable as they are emphatic. Sears Tower is well loved not only because the city looks up to it in awe, but because it looks back at the city as well. From Sears Tower, Chicago is an equally awesome sight to behold. Perhaps it is just this relationship that explains the nobility and prestige of Sears Tower. As Chicago grows in size and substance, so does the stature of the 1,454-foot behemoth that invites everyone in the world to the top.

Enormous spans of space are one of the challenges where, for the offices of
Ernst and Young, the Environments Group created a flowing interior that
contradicted the rectilinear modernism of the building when it was built.

Photograph © Hedrich Blessing

As the spiritual center of twentieth-century American architecture, Chicago's Sears Tower denies the view that modernism has made U.S. cities all the same. All great skyscrapers have personalities and profiles all their own. Chicago has at least three, including the Aon Building (middle) and John Hancock (right) that are among America's most recognizable architectural monuments.